AF428707

"We can't solve problems by using
the same kind of thinking we used
when we created them."

— Albert Einstein

Come evolve with us.

The challenges of the 21st century won't be solved with a traditional leadership approach. It will be solved by leaders who are willing to learn, unlearn, and relearn.

Dr. Robyn Short, CEO
Workplace Peace Institute

Workplace Peace Institute Leadership Academy exists to support leaders in honoring basic human needs and dignity needs, creating a paradigm shift for the 21st century workplace.

The WPI Leadership Academy bridges scholarly expertise with experiential, brain-based learning in an online, self-paced format with opportunities for live virtual learning and community building designed for today's busy professional. Our courses support existing and emerging leaders in embracing the skills and competencies necessary to actualize human potential in a constantly changing world and workplace.

Workplace Peace Institute Leadership Academy optimizes competencies in Leadership Intelligences, New Paradigm Leadership, Communication Skills, Conflict Resolution, and Diversity, Equity, Inclusion and Belonging to create highly engaged workplaces where all people thrive.

WPI LEADERSHIP ACADEMY BENEFITS

Our courses meet the criteria for SHRM and HRCI recertification credits.

Unlimited Access to Your Courses: Unlike many online educational courses, WPI Leadership Academy gives you unlimited access to your course. You can access your course whenever you want for as long as you want. Course access is not restricted to a three- to six-month period.

Monthly Live Virtual Learning Sessions: As a Workplace Peace Institute Leadership Academy learner you have access to monthly live virtual learning sessions. These virtual learning sessions are intended to support your on-going professional development and also provide an opportunity for you to collaborate and network with professionals who share your interest in cultivating new paradigm leadership skills.

Community of Practice: Workplace Peace Institute Leadership Academy invites learners to join the Leadership

Academy Community of Practice. This online community is for professionals who share a passion for actualizing human potential through a new paradigm leadership model. The Community of Practice is designed to engage in relationship building, discussion, and activities particularly as it relates to the knowledge, skills, and practices gained in the WPI Leadership Academy.

Mobile-Access to All Content: The mobile app gives you access to online courses, educational resources, to the live virtual learning sessions and other events, as well as the Community of Practice.

Dedicated Engagement Manager: Your course is supported by a Leadership Academy Engagement Manager. The Engagement Manager works with you to ensure you get the most out of your courses. The Engagement Manager will communicate with you and encourage you as you work through each module and the corresponding activities and help you deepen your learning experience. While the Engagement Manager will reach out to you to support you, you can also reach out to them any time with questions.

Reimagine work with us! Explore our course offerings at **www.workplacepeaceinstitute.com**

New paradigm leaders prioritize the well-being of people and communities in ways that have lasting, intrinsic value.

Date   /   /

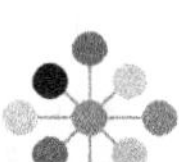

New paradigm leaders share power, putting those closest to a problem closest to the solution.

New paradigm leaders cultivate collaboration. Leadership is exercised through respectful dialogue, transparent knowledge-sharing, and partnership.

Date   /   /

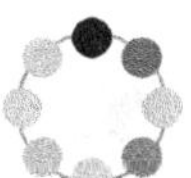

New paradigm leaders encourage leadership to be exercised by
everyone at all levels of the organization.

New paradigm leaders focus on serving all stakeholders of the organization or community.

Date   /   /

New paradigm leaders succeed by loving and caring for coworkers, customers, and everyone else who contributes to the enterprise, including their competitors.

New paradigm leaders ensure everyone is subject to the same rules of behavior, processes, and reward systems.

Date   /   /

New paradigm leaders value diversity, equity, inclusion, and belonging.

New paradigm leaders prioritize transparency, ensuring information
is shared openly with all levels of the organization.

Date   /   /

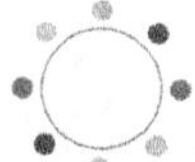

New paradigm leaders ensure groups participate together in planning and carrying out changes that affect them, guided by shared whole-system knowledge.

New paradigm leaders prioritize the well-being of people and communities in ways that have lasting, intrinsic value.

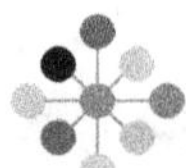

New paradigm leaders share power, putting those closest to a problem closest to the solution.

New paradigm leaders cultivate collaboration. Leadership is exercised through respectful dialogue, transparent knowledge-sharing, and partnership.

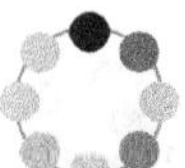

New paradigm leaders encourage leadership to be exercised by
everyone at all levels of the organization.

New paradigm leaders focus on serving all stakeholders of the
organization or community.

Date   /   /

New paradigm leaders succeed by loving and caring for coworkers, customers, and everyone else who contributes to the enterprise, including their competitors.

New paradigm leaders ensure everyone is subject to the same rules of behavior, processes, and reward systems.

New paradigm leaders value diversity, equity, inclusion, and belonging.

New paradigm leaders prioritize transparency, ensuring information
is shared openly with all levels of the organization.

Date   /   /

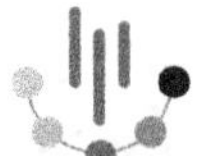

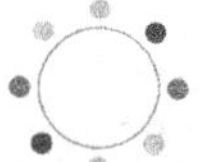

New paradigm leaders ensure groups participate together in planning and carrying out changes that affect them, guided by shared whole-system knowledge.

New paradigm leaders prioritize the well-being of people and
communities in ways that have lasting, intrinsic value.

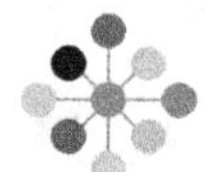

New paradigm leaders share power, putting those closest to a problem closest to the solution.

New paradigm leaders cultivate collaboration. Leadership is exercised through respectful dialogue, transparent knowledge-sharing, and partnership.

Date   /   /

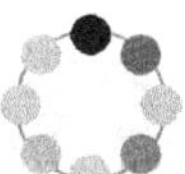

New paradigm leaders encourage leadership to be exercised by everyone at all levels of the organization.

New paradigm leaders focus on serving all stakeholders of the
organization or community.

Date   /   /

New paradigm leaders succeed by loving and caring for coworkers, customers, and everyone else who contributes to the enterprise, including their competitors.

New paradigm leaders ensure everyone is subject to the same rules of
behavior, processes, and reward systems.

New paradigm leaders prioritize transparency, ensuring information
is shared openly with all levels of the organization.

New paradigm leaders ensure groups participate together in planning and carrying out changes that affect them, guided by shared whole-system knowledge.

New paradigm leaders prioritize the well-being of people and communities in ways that have lasting, intrinsic value.

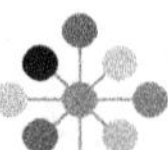

New paradigm leaders cultivate collaboration. Leadership is exercised through respectful dialogue, transparent knowledge-sharing, and partnership.

Date   /   /

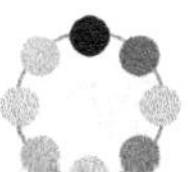

New paradigm leaders encourage leadership to be exercised by
everyone at all levels of the organization.

New paradigm leaders focus on serving all stakeholders of the organization or community.

Date   /   /

New paradigm leaders succeed by loving and caring for coworkers, customers, and everyone else who contributes to the enterprise, including their competitors.

New paradigm leaders ensure everyone is subject to the same rules of behavior, processes, and reward systems.

Date   /   /

New paradigm leaders prioritize transparency, ensuring information is shared openly with all levels of the organization.

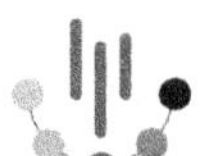

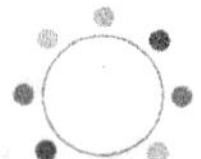

New paradigm leaders ensure groups participate together in planning and carrying out changes that affect them, guided by shared whole-system knowledge.

New paradigm leaders prioritize the well-being of people and communities in ways that have lasting, intrinsic value.

New paradigm leaders share power, putting those closest to a problem closest to the solution.

New paradigm leaders cultivate collaboration. Leadership is exercised through respectful dialogue, transparent knowledge-sharing, and partnership.

Date   /   /

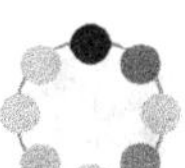

New paradigm leaders focus on serving all stakeholders of the
organization or community.

Date   /   /

New paradigm leaders succeed by loving and caring for coworkers, customers, and everyone else who contributes to the enterprise, including their competitors.

New paradigm leaders ensure everyone is subject to the same rules of behavior, processes, and reward systems.

Date   /   /

New paradigm leaders prioritize transparency, ensuring information
is shared openly with all levels of the organization.

Date   /   /

New paradigm leaders ensure groups participate together in planning and carrying out changes that affect them, guided by shared whole-system knowledge.

New paradigm leaders prioritize the well-being of people and communities in ways that have lasting, intrinsic value.

Date   /   /

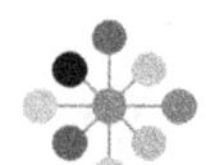

New paradigm leaders share power, putting those closest to a
problem closest to the solution.

New paradigm leaders cultivate collaboration. Leadership is exercised through respectful dialogue, transparent knowledge-sharing, and partnership.

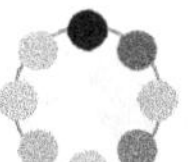

New paradigm leaders encourage leadership to be exercised by everyone at all levels of the organization.

New paradigm leaders focus on serving all stakeholders of the
organization or community.

Date   /   /

New paradigm leaders succeed by loving and caring for coworkers, customers, and everyone else who contributes to the enterprise, including their competitors.

New paradigm leaders ensure everyone is subject to the same rules of behavior, processes, and reward systems.

Date   /   /

New paradigm leaders prioritize transparency, ensuring information is shared openly with all levels of the organization.

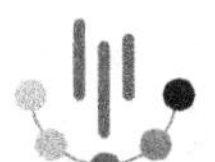

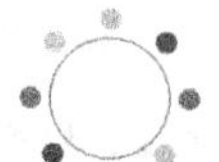

New paradigm leaders ensure groups participate together in planning and carrying out changes that affect them, guided by shared whole-system knowledge.

New paradigm leaders prioritize the well-being of people and communities in ways that have lasting, intrinsic value.

www.workplacepeaceinstitute.com

www.ingramcontent.com/pod-product-compliance
Lightning Source LLC
Chambersburg PA
CBHW071542120726
48009CB00002B/55